Patterns Outside

Daniel Nunn

Raintree

Chicago, Illinois

www.capstonepub.com
Visit our website to find out more information about Heinemann-Raintree books.

To order:
☎ Phone 800-747-4992
🖥 Visit www.capstonepub.com to browse our catalog and order online.

Edited by Daniel Nunn, Rebecca Rissman, and Sian Smith
Designed by Joanna Hinton-Malivoire
Picture research by Elizabeth Alexander
Illustrations by Joanna Hinton-Malivoire
Originated by Capstone Global Library Ltd.
Production by Victoria Fitzgerald

Library of Congress Cataloging-in-Publication Data
Nunn, Daniel.
    Patterns outside / Daniel Nunn.
        p. cm. – (Math every day)
    Includes bibliographical references and index.
    ISBN 978-1-4329-5731-5 (hb) – ISBN 978-1-4329-5736-0 (pb)
    1. Shapes–Juvenile literature. 2. Mathematics in nature–Juvenile literature. I. Title.
    QA445.5.N855 2012
    516'.15–dc23
                                2011013019

Acknowledgments
We would like to thank the following for permission to reproduce photographs: Shutterstock pp.4 (© Dmitry Naumov), 5 (© Travis Klein), 6 (© Glenn Young), 7 (© Mark Bridger), 8 (© Studio Araminta), 9 (© Peter Waters), 10 (© Kamira), 11 (© Jim Barber), 12 (© Chunni4691), 13 (© Larry Ye), 14 (© clearviewstock), 15 (© VVO), 16 (© Goncharuk), 17 (© Christopher Penler), 18 (© SVLuma), 19 (© Anthony Hall), 20 (© tan4ikk), 21 (© Elena Elisseeva).

Cover photograph of a butterfly on flowers reproduced with permission of Shutterstock (© Bershadsky Yuri). Back cover photograph of rain drops rippling in a puddle reproduced with permission of Shutterstock (© Dmitry Naumov); tracks in the snow Shutterstock (© Travis Klein).

Every effort has been made to contact copyright holders of any material reproduced in this book. Any omissions will be rectified in subsequent printings if notice is given to the publisher.

Contents

Patterns Outside

There are patterns everywhere we go.

In the rain and in the snow.

Patterns in Nature

These birds make a pattern in the sky.

These swans line up
as they waddle by.

7

This snail has a spiral on its shell.

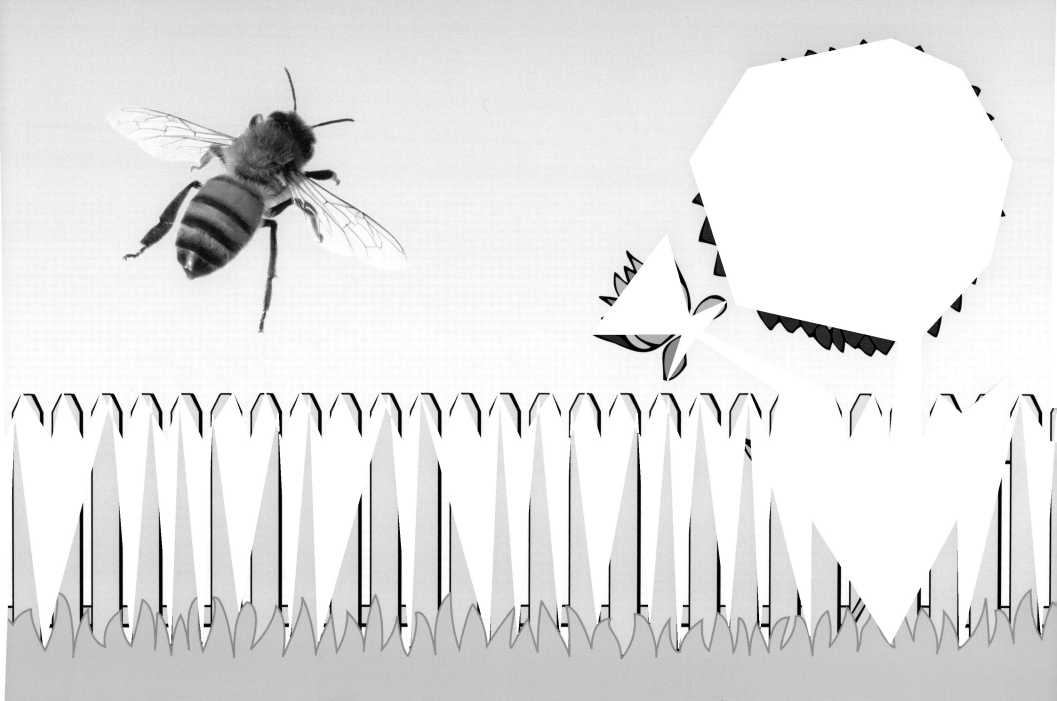

This bee is striped,
can you tell?

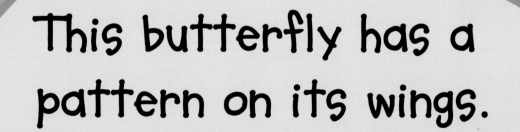

This butterfly has a pattern on its wings.

This tree trunk's pattern is shaped like rings.

These patterned leaves are
on a plant called clover.

This spider's web
has dew all over.

Patterns Made by People

Patterns are made by people, too.

This patterned fence is in a zoo!

Can you see the patterns in this wall?

16

Or in these buildings, oh so tall?

Can you find the patterns painted on this street?

Or the patterns on this lawn?
It's tidy and neat!

There are patterns on
the clothes we wear.

Yes, there are patterns EVERYWHERE!

Complete the Patterns

Can you work out what's missing from the patterns here?

?

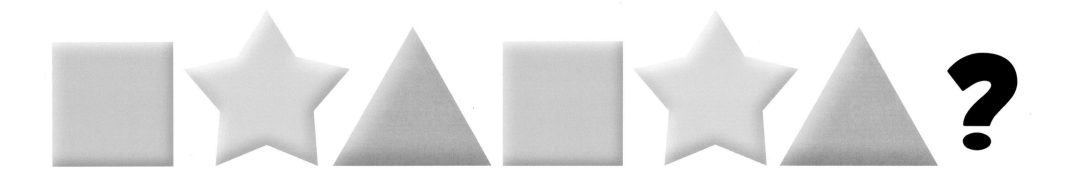

If you get both patterns right,
we'll give you a cheer!

Answers on page 24

Index

Answer to quiz on page 22:

The missing shape is a blue triangle.

Answer to quiz on page 23:

The missing shape is a green square.